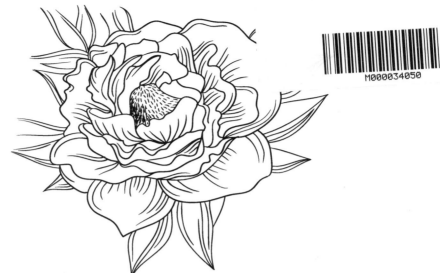

Promises
of
God

Bible Verses to Color

Coloring Quotes
Adult Coloring Book

xist Publishing

Want to hear about more coloring quotes books?

Visit xistpublishing.com/color

to sign up for our Coloring Quotes newsletter and get a free
exclusive printable coloring page.

Bible Verses are from the Open English Bible
Designed by Calee M. Lee
with images from Fotolia
Design Copyright © 2016 Calee M. Lee
This collection may be photocopied for classroom and
individual use only. Please do not reproduce and post
on the Internet, email to all of your friends, or reuse
the designs in this book in any way for commercial or
personal profit.
ISBN: 978-1-5324-0013-1
Published by Xist Publishing in 2016
PO Box 61593, Irvine CA 92602
www.xistpublishing.com

He who began a GOOD WORK in you will COMPLETE it

Phil 1:6

If anyone is in union with Christ, he is a new being!

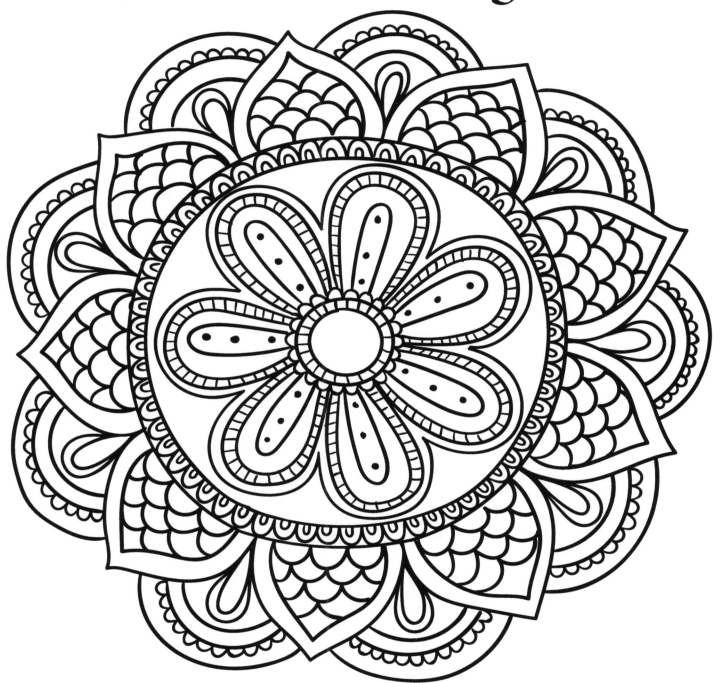

His old life has passed away; a new life has begun!

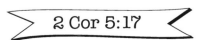

2 Cor 5:17

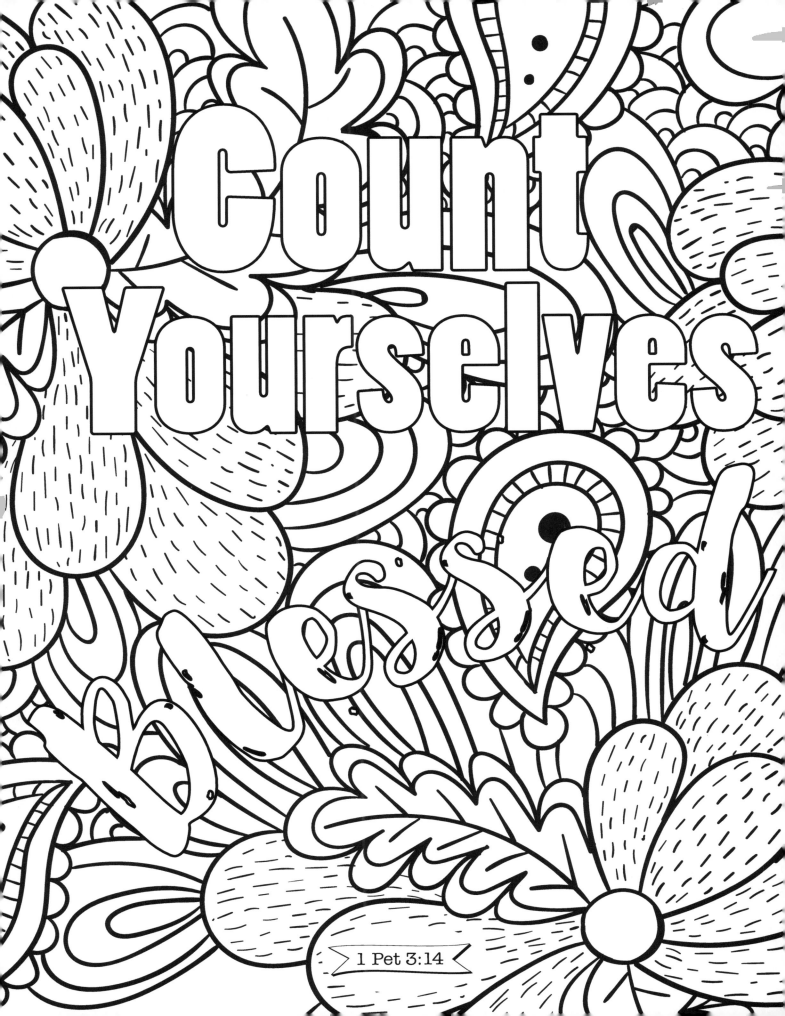

Count Yourselves Blessed

1 Pet 3:14

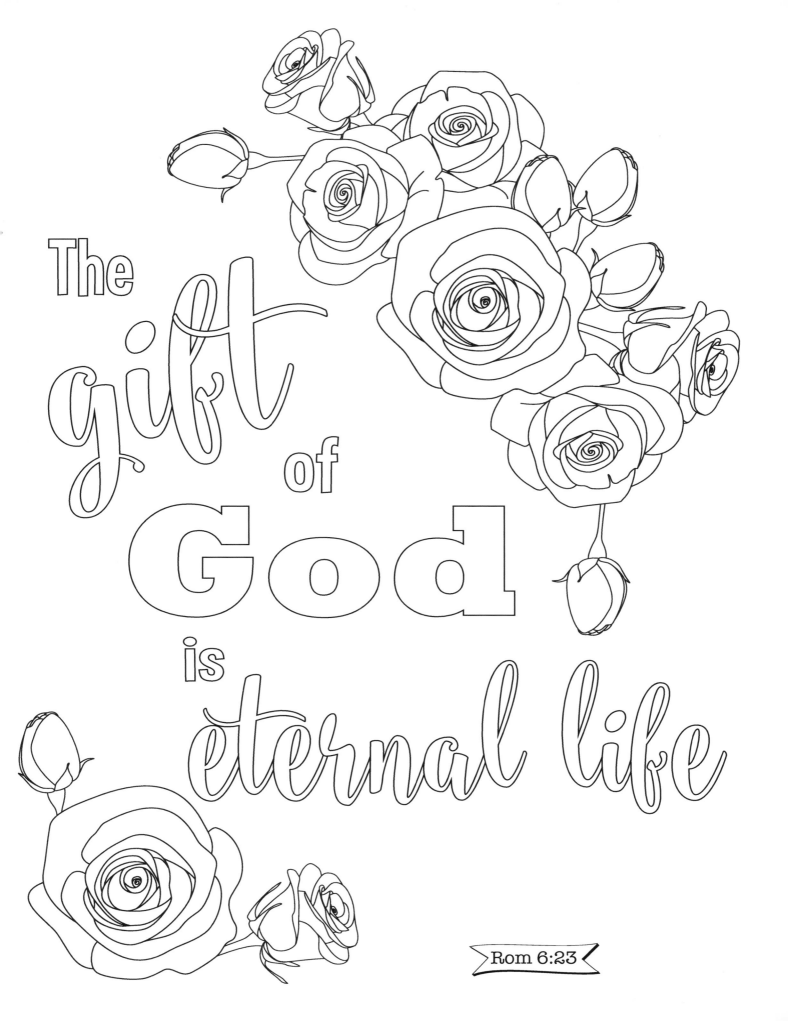

The gift of God is eternal life

Rom 6:23

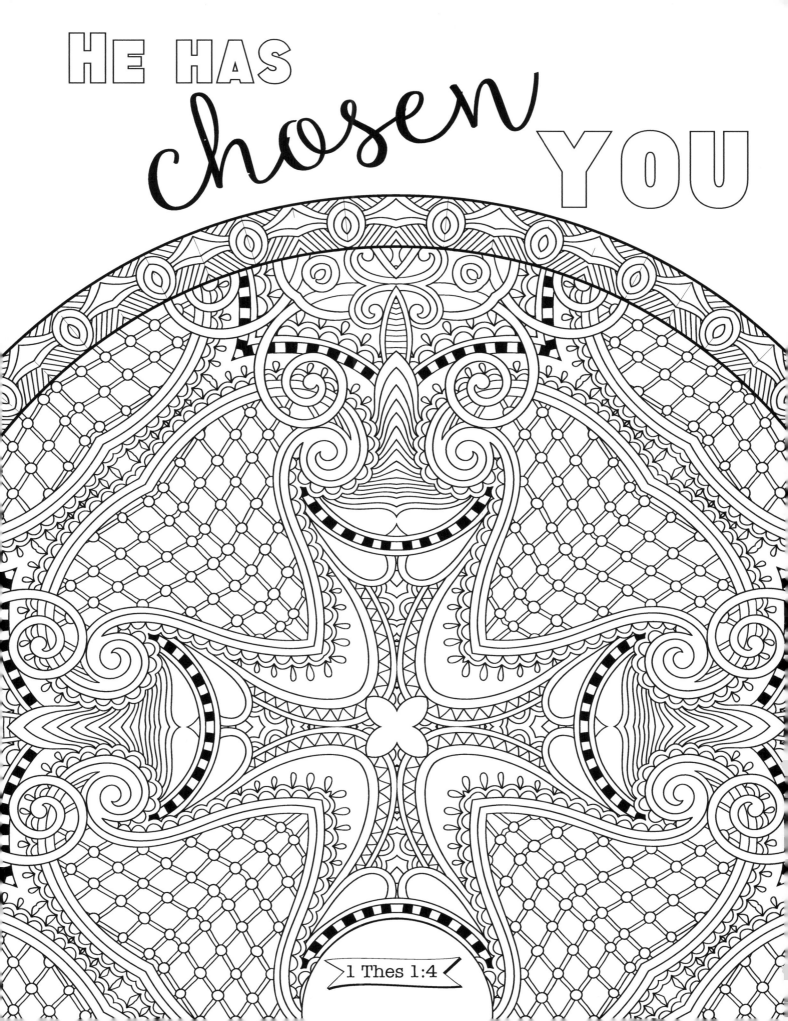

He has *chosen* YOU

1 Thes 1:4

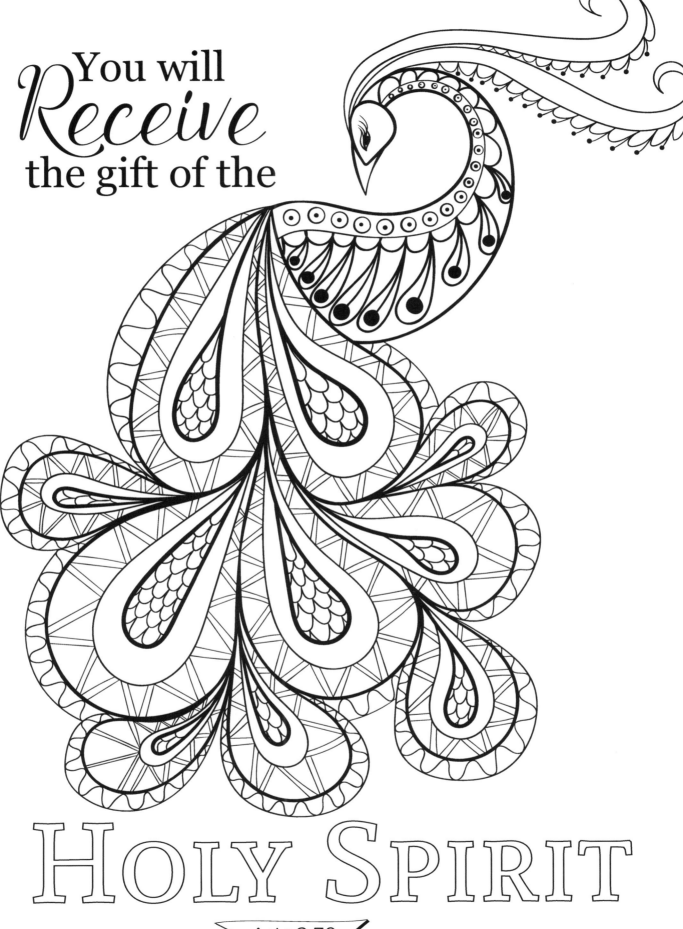

You will *Receive* the gift of the

HOLY SPIRIT

Acts 2:38

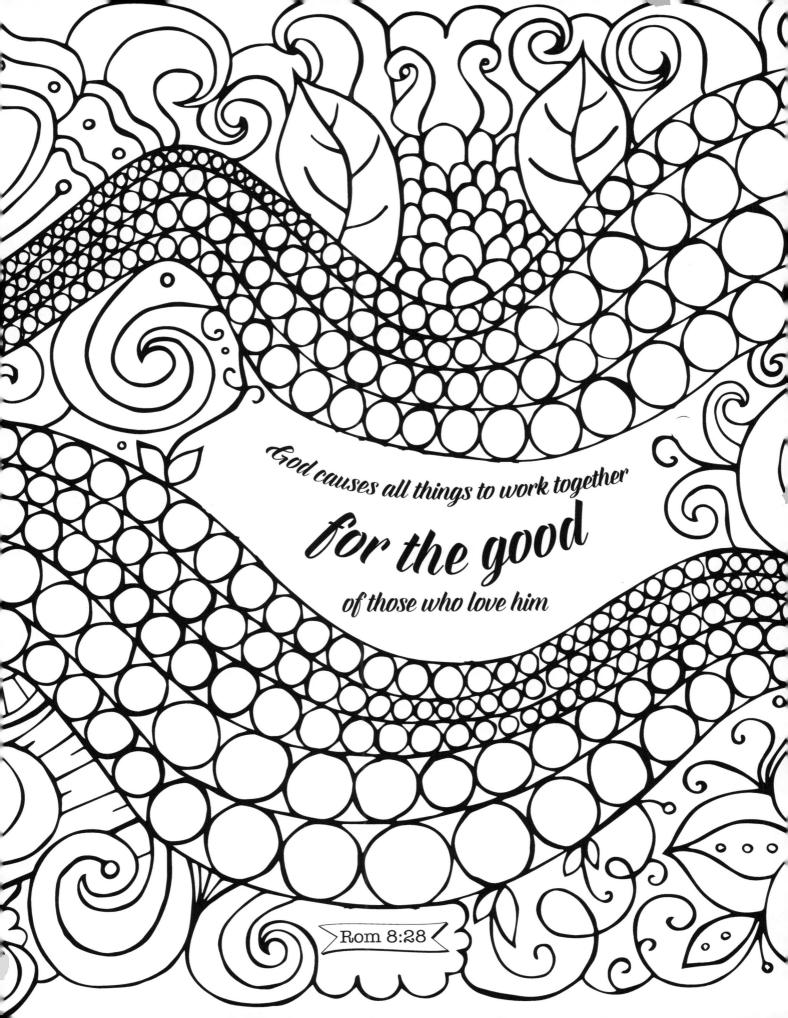

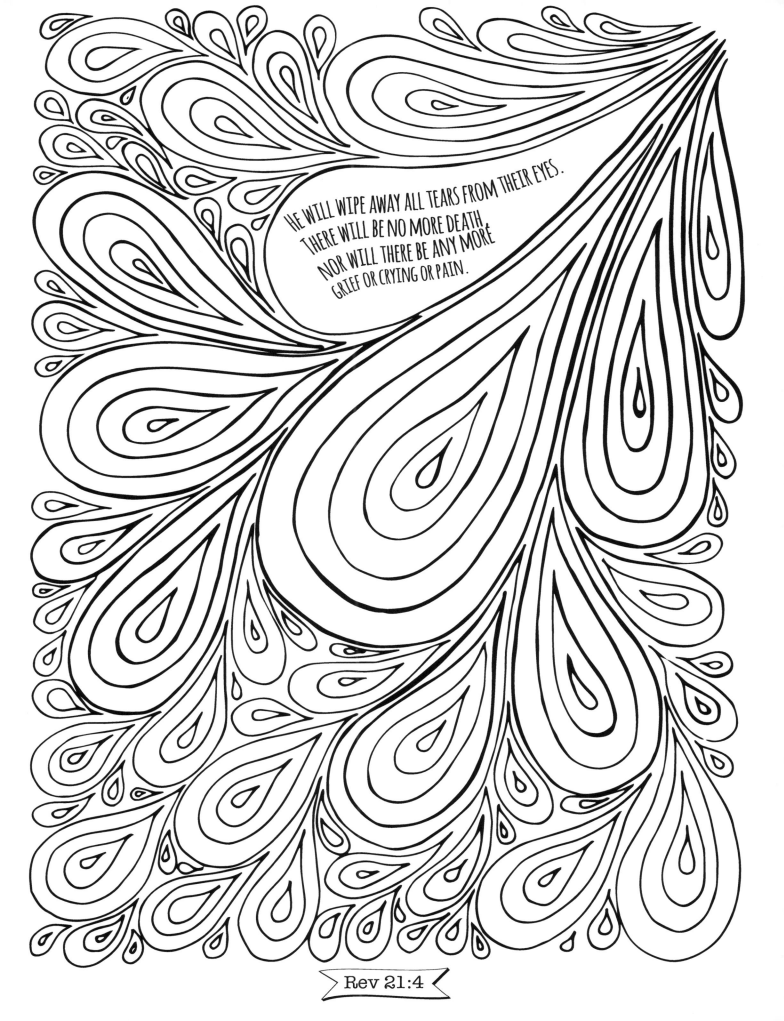

He will wipe away all tears from their eyes. There will be no more death, nor will there be any more grief or crying or pain.

Rev 21:4

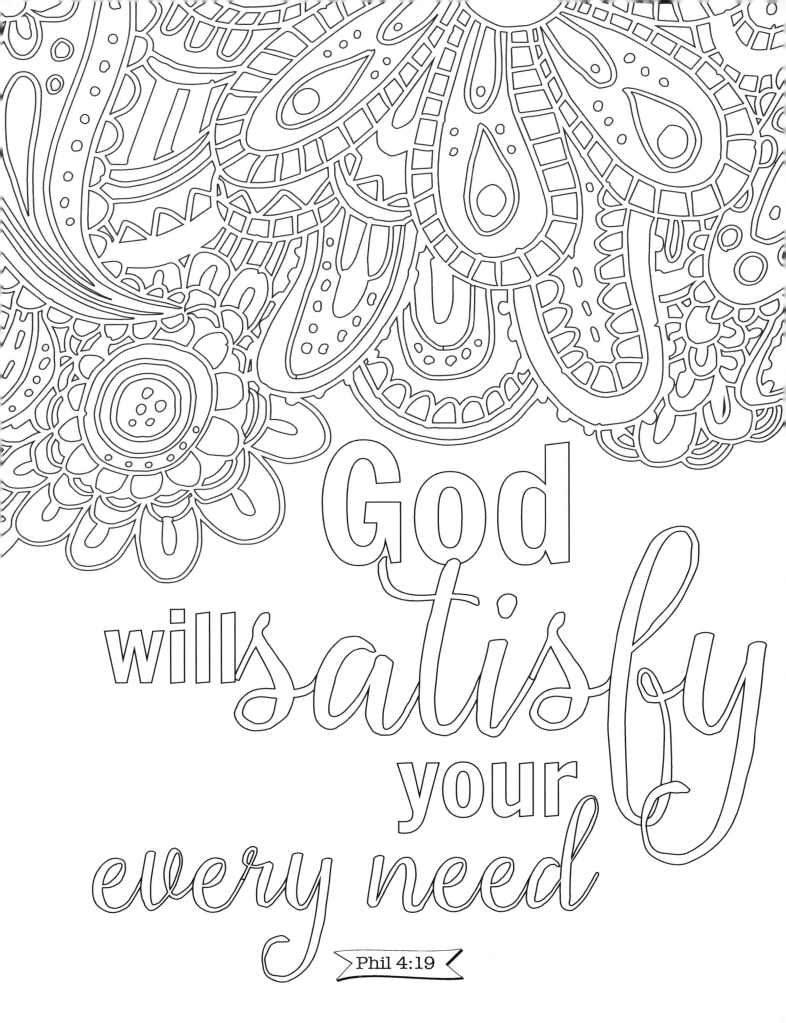

God will satisfy your every need

Phil 4:19

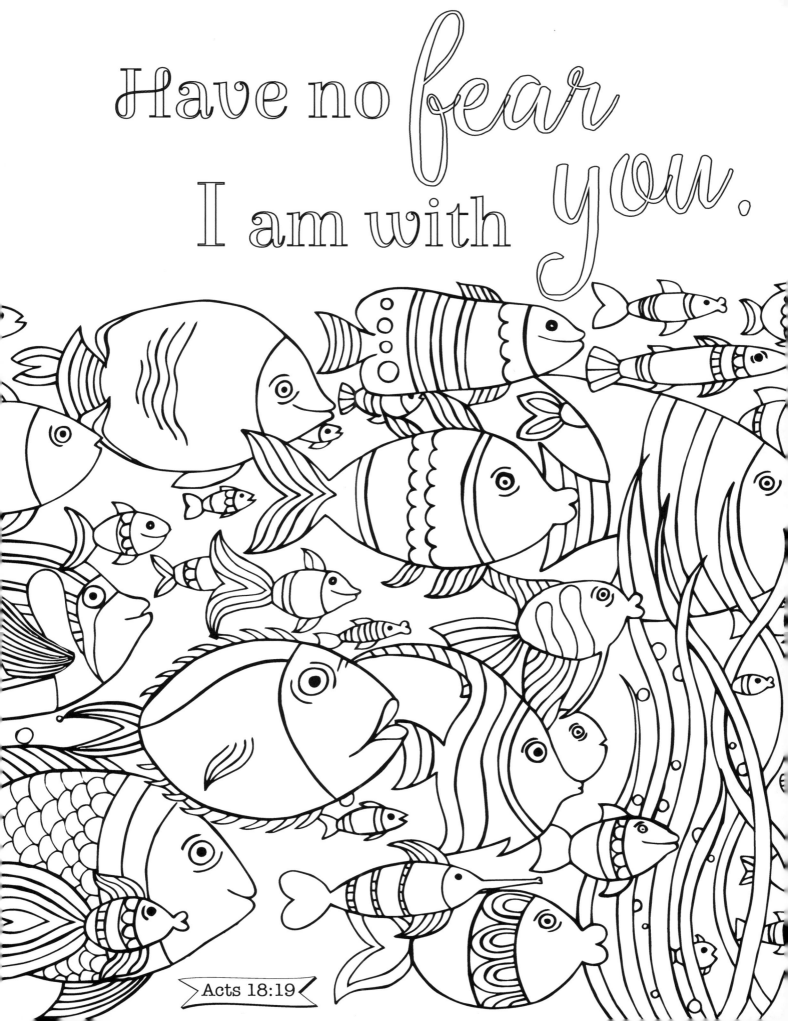

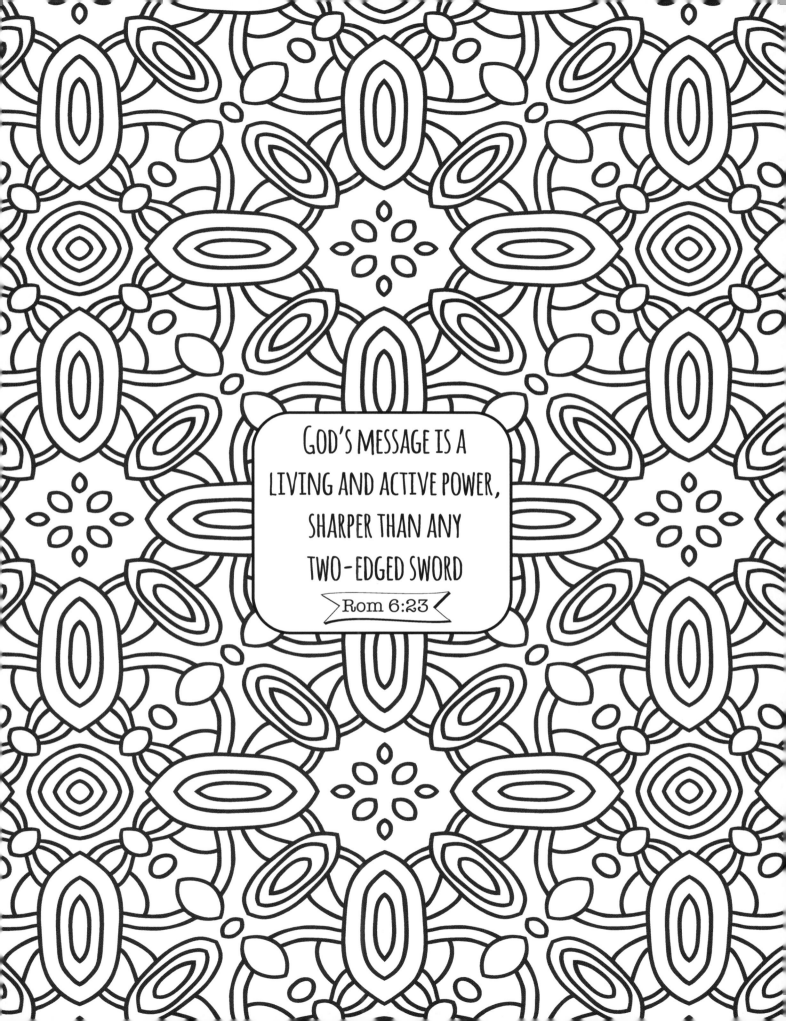

God's message is a living and active power, sharper than any two-edged sword

Rom 6:23

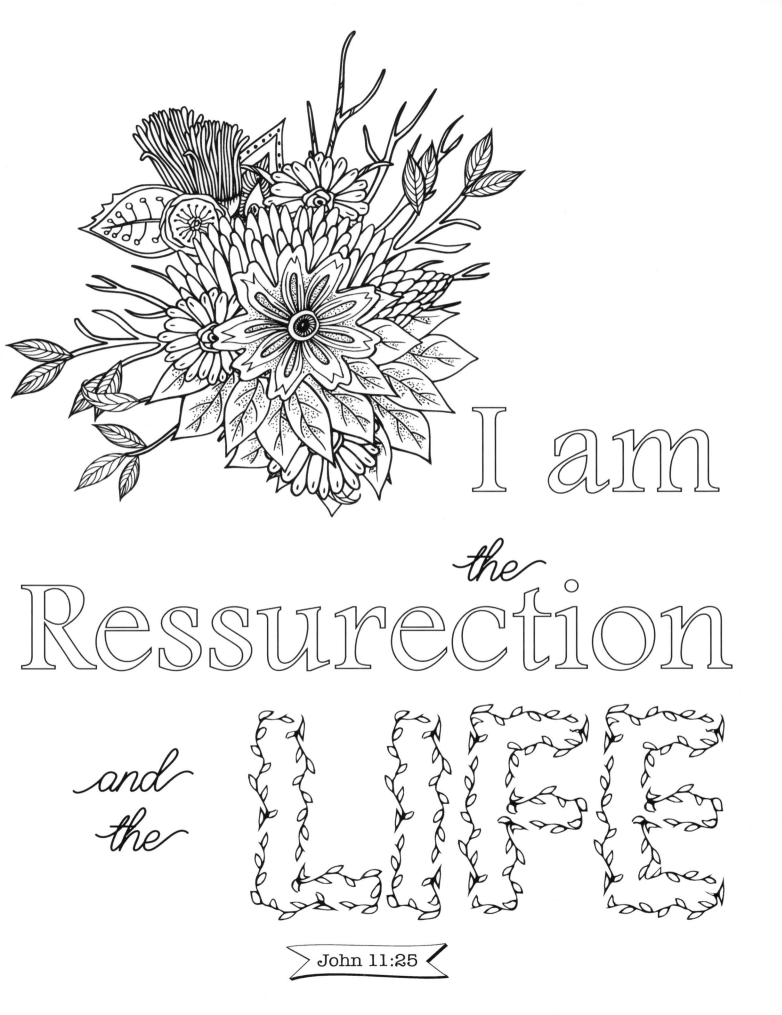

I am the Ressurection and the LIFE

John 11:25

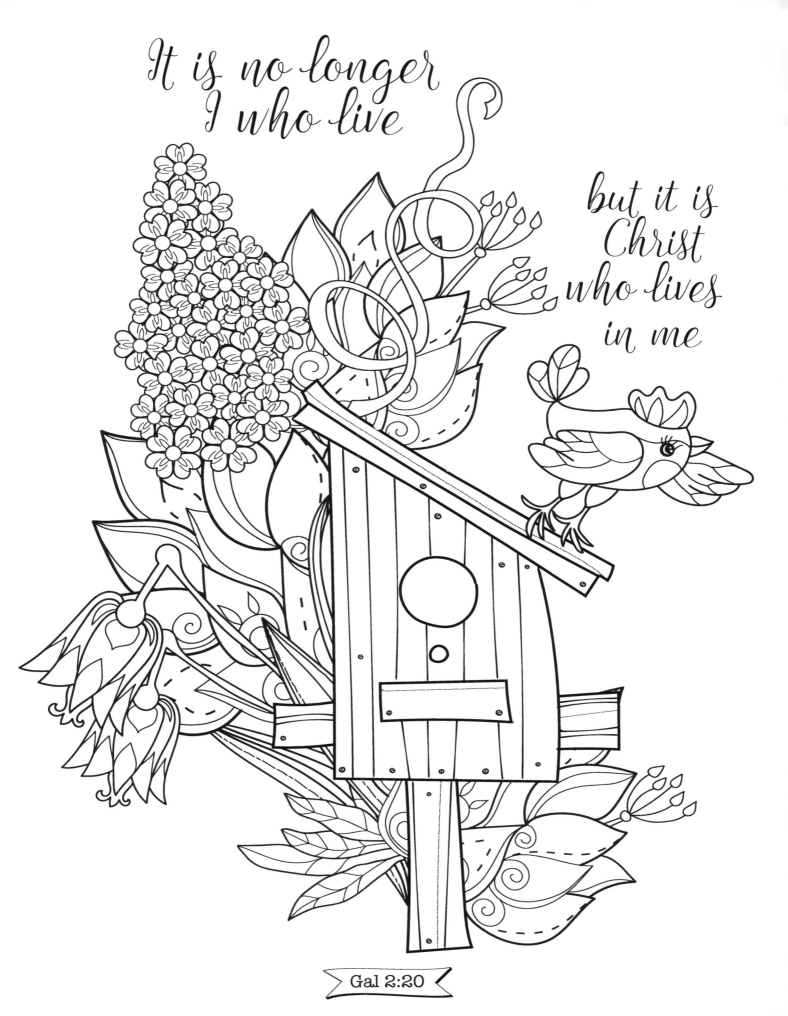

It is no longer I who live

but it is Christ who lives in me

Gal 2:20

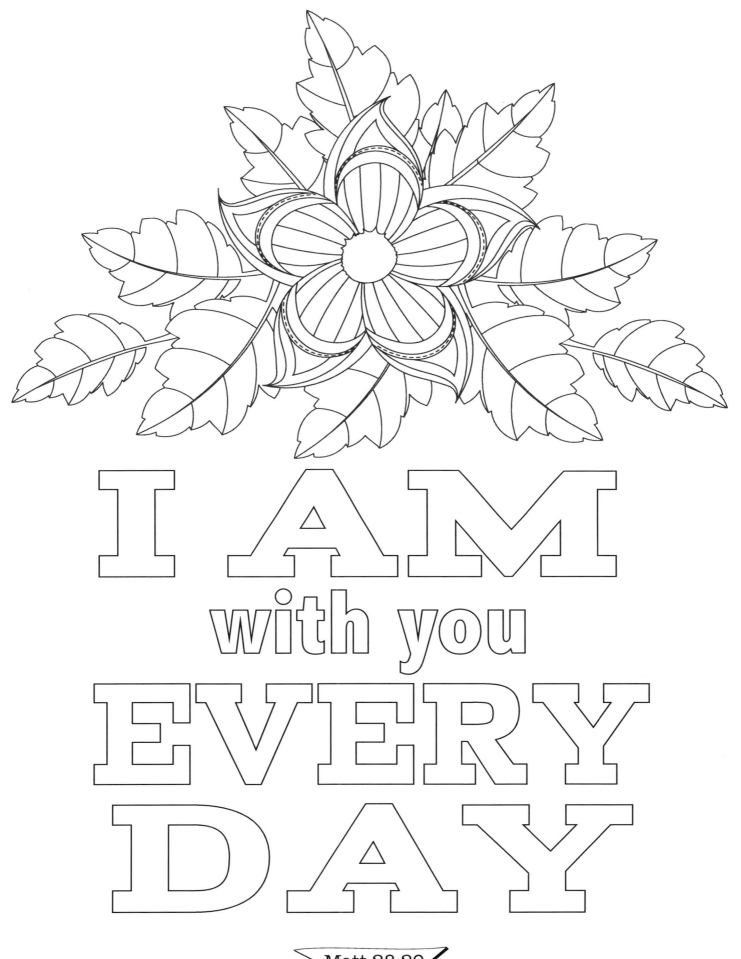

I AM
with you
EVERY
DAY

Matt 28:20

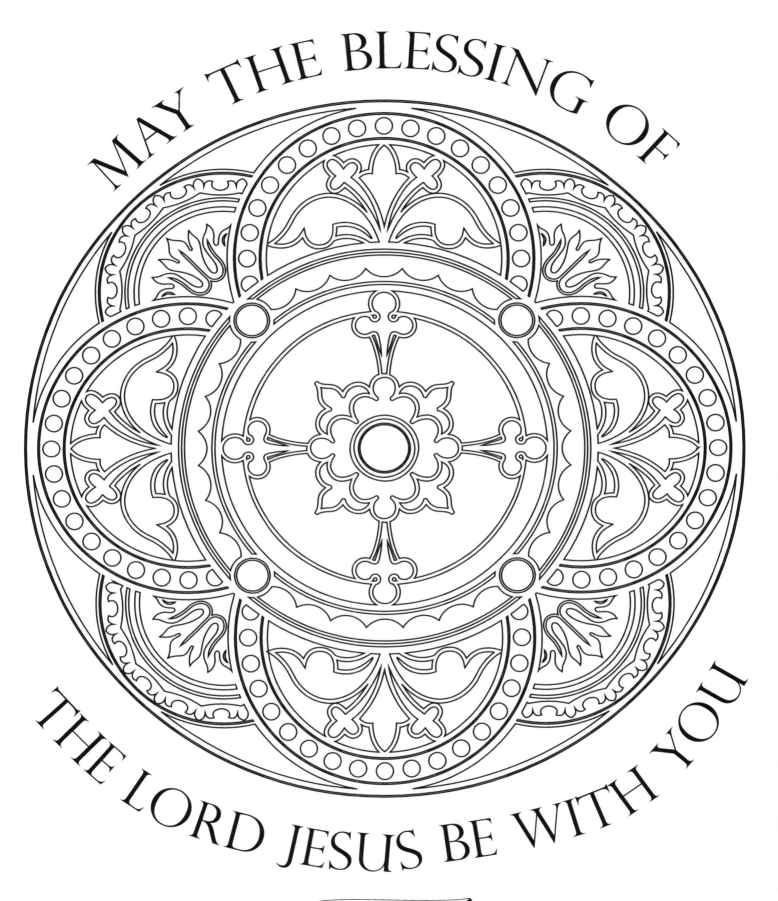

MAY THE BLESSING OF

THE LORD JESUS BE WITH YOU

1 Cor 16:24

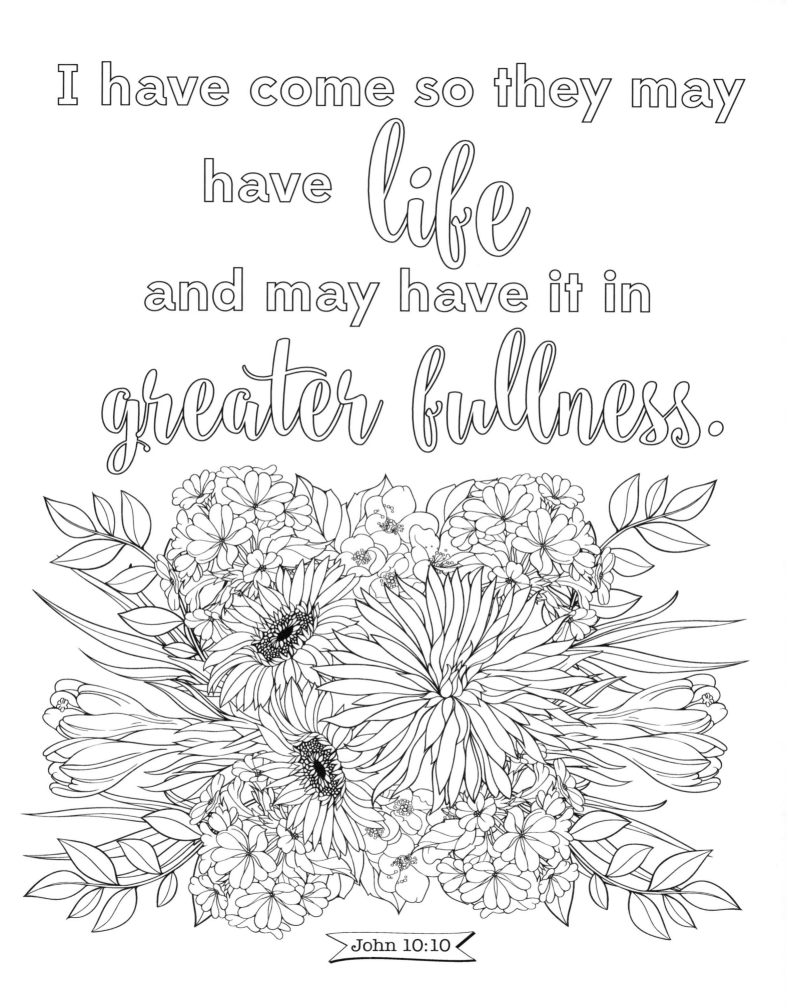

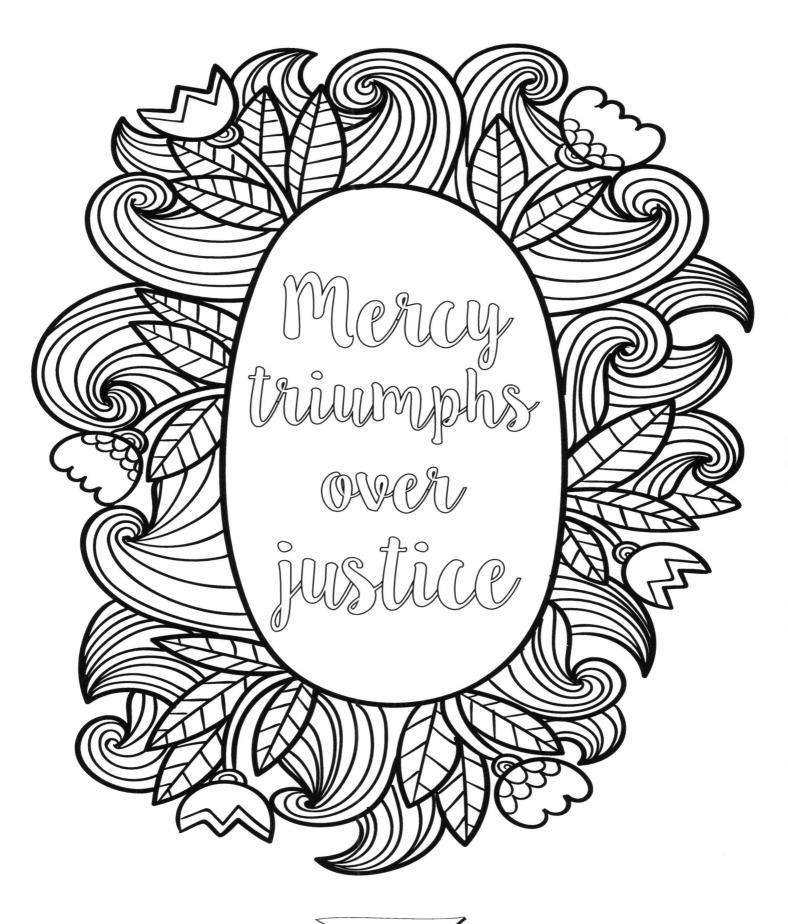

Mercy triumphs over justice

Heb 2:13

I myself am with you

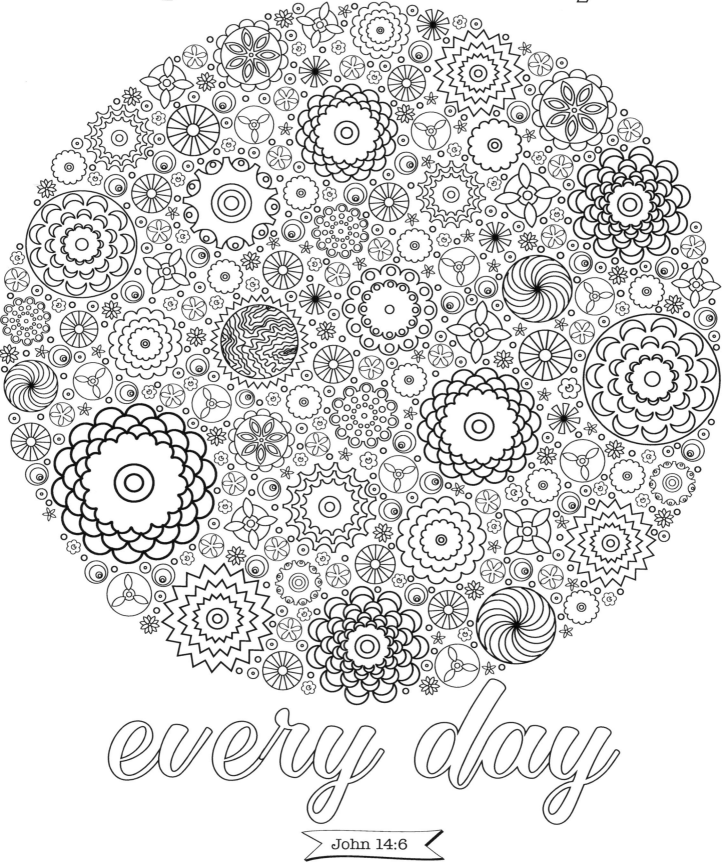

every day

John 14:6

My help is ENOUGH for you

2 Cor 12:19

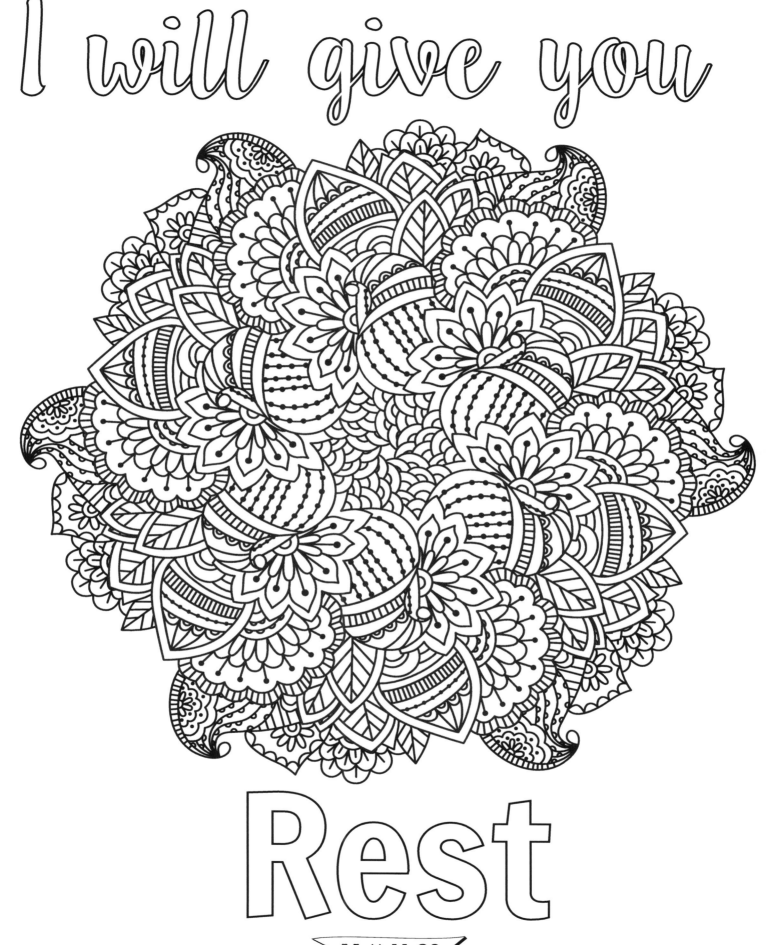

I will give you

Rest

Matt 11:28

In the world you will find trouble; yet,
take courage! I have conquered the world

John 16:23

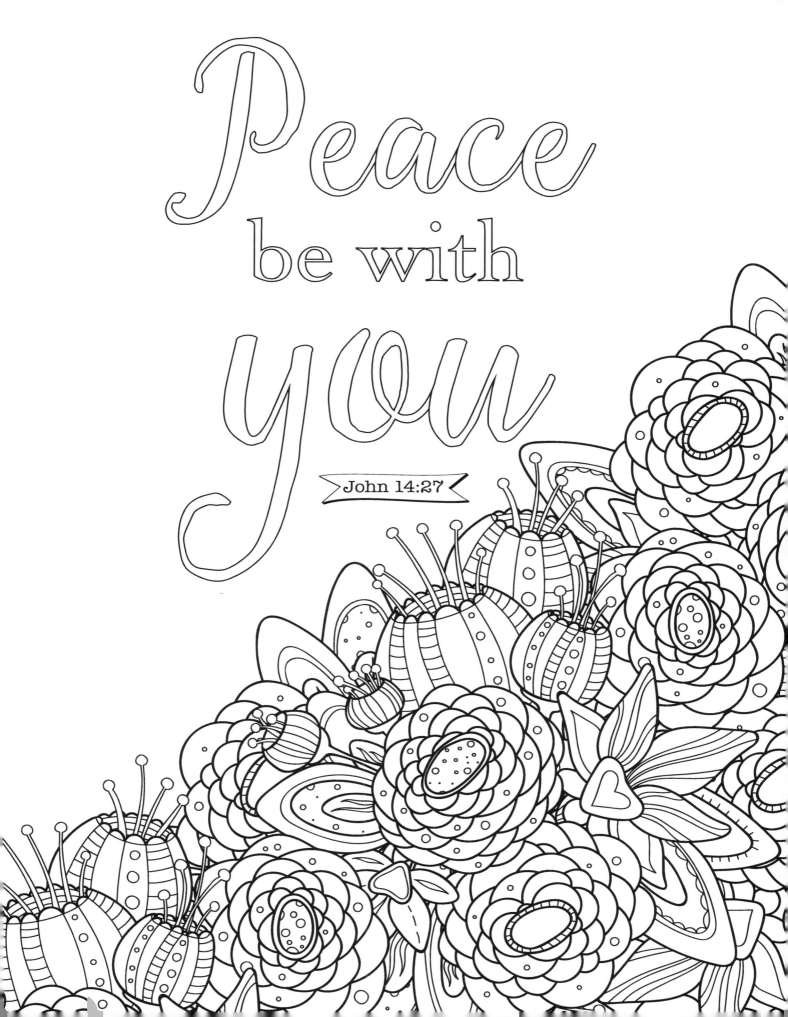

Peace
be with
you

John 14:27

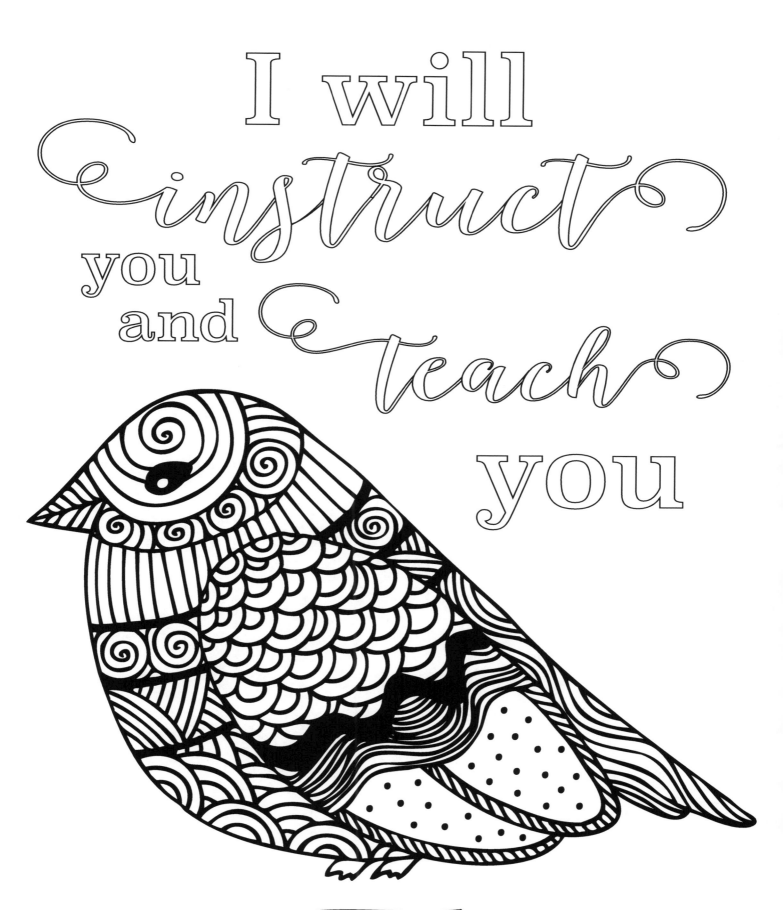

I will instruct you and teach you

Psalm 32:8

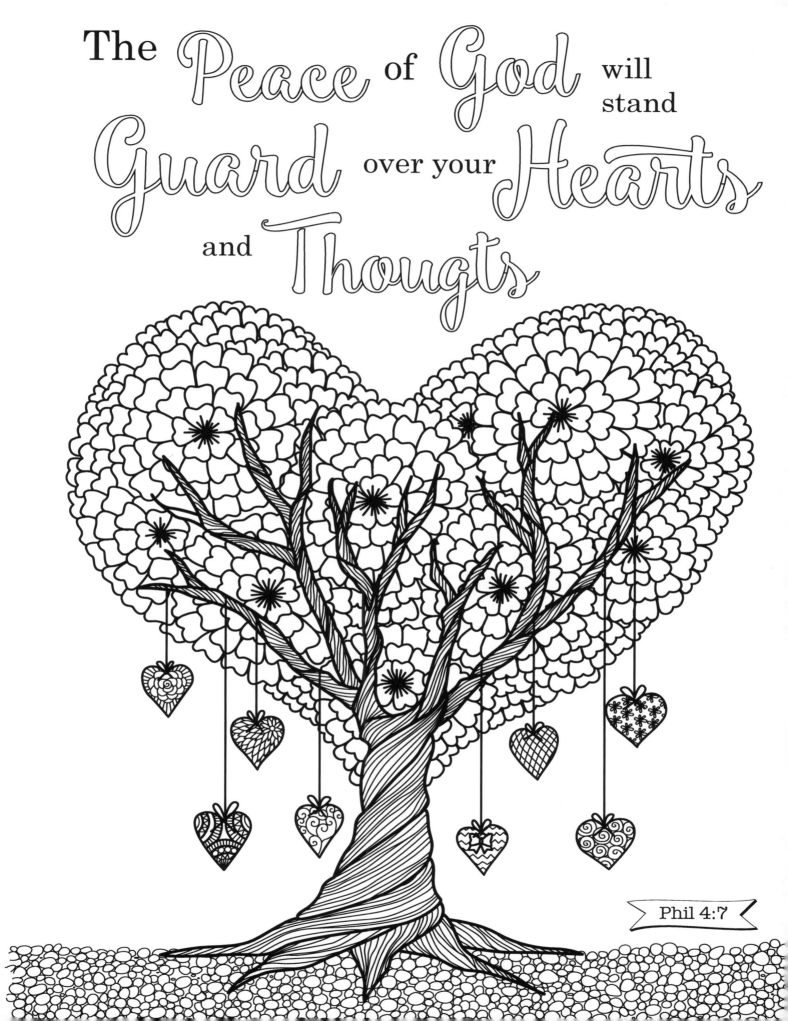

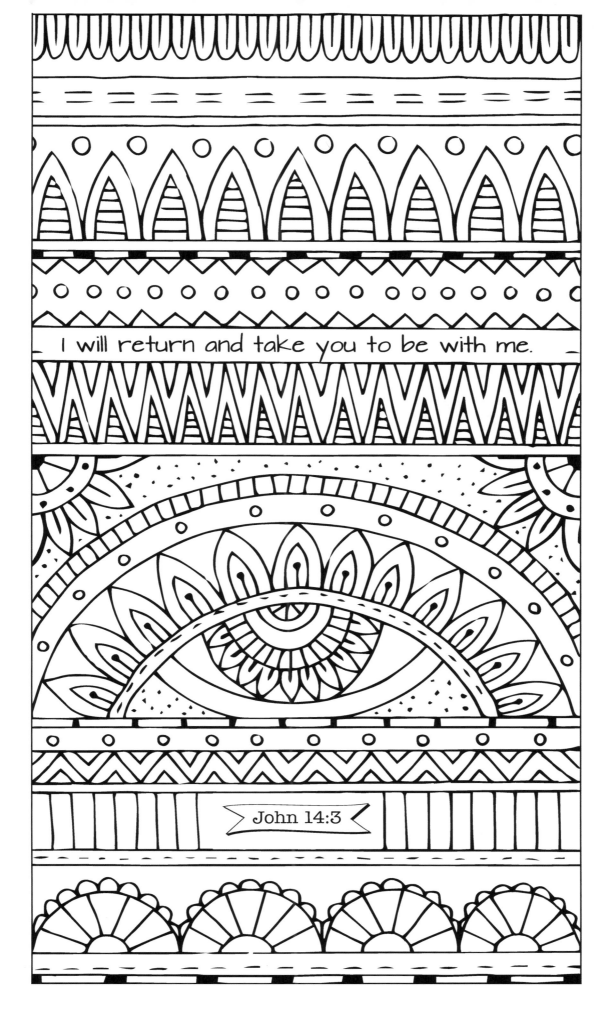

I will return and take you to be with me.

John 14:3

What is impossible with people

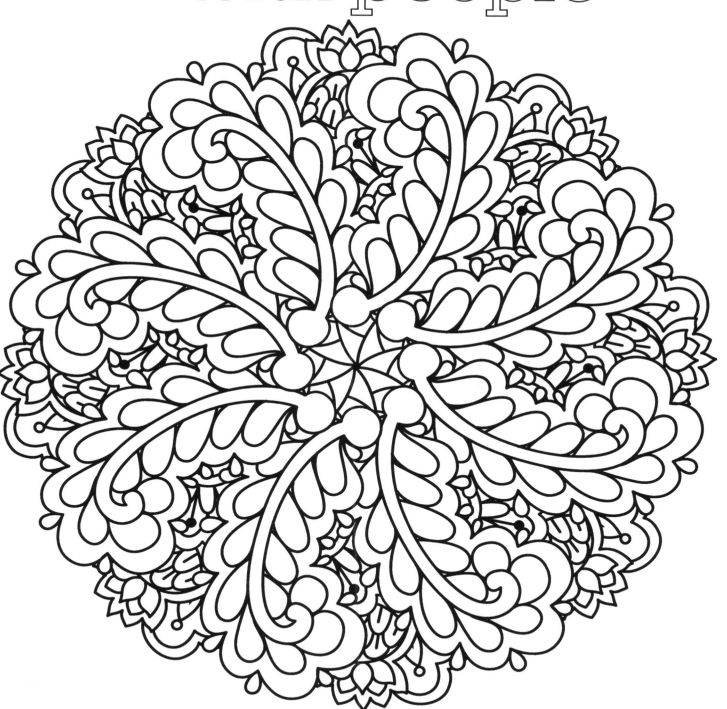

is possible with God

Luke 18:27

The Lord will guard your *comings and goings* from now and for *evermore*

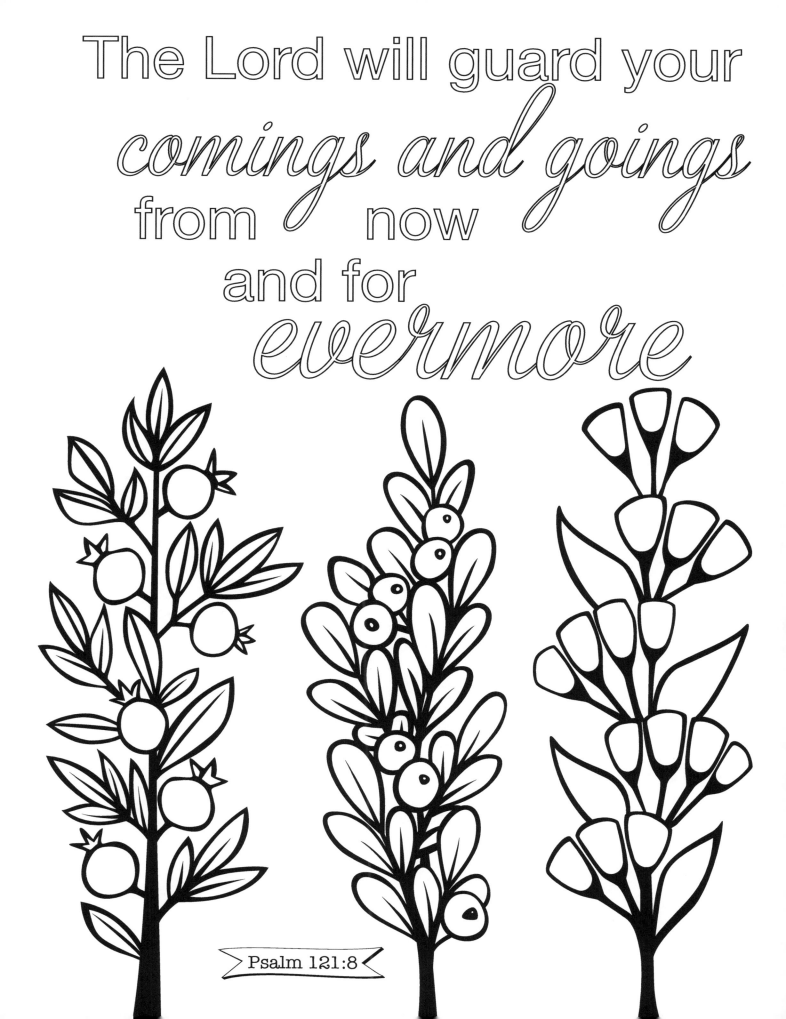

Psalm 121:8

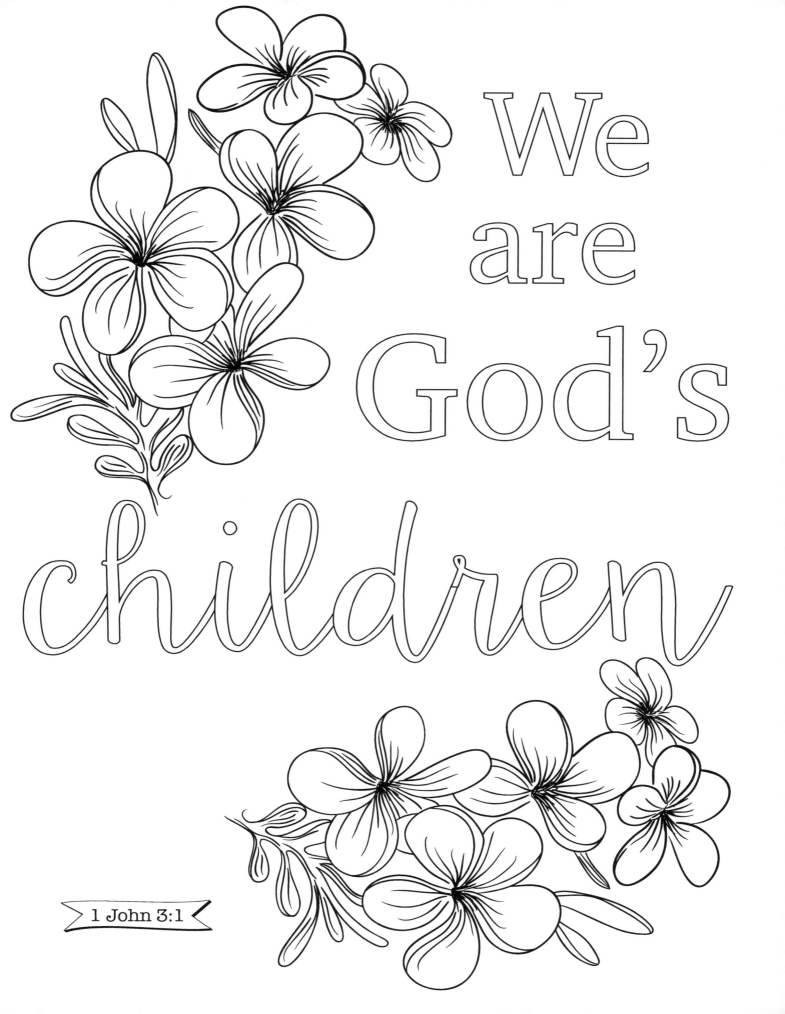

We are God's
HANDIWORK

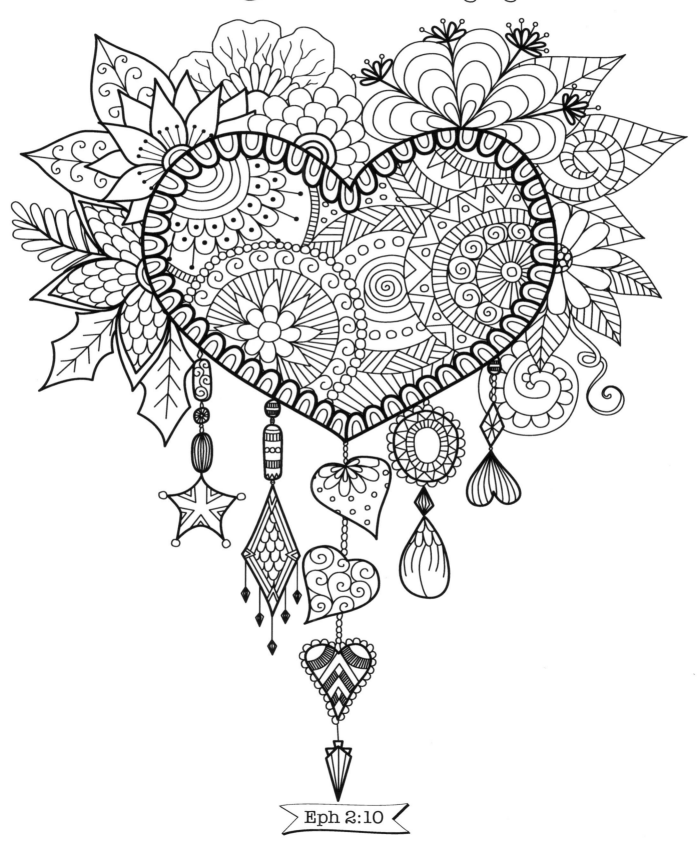

Eph 2:10

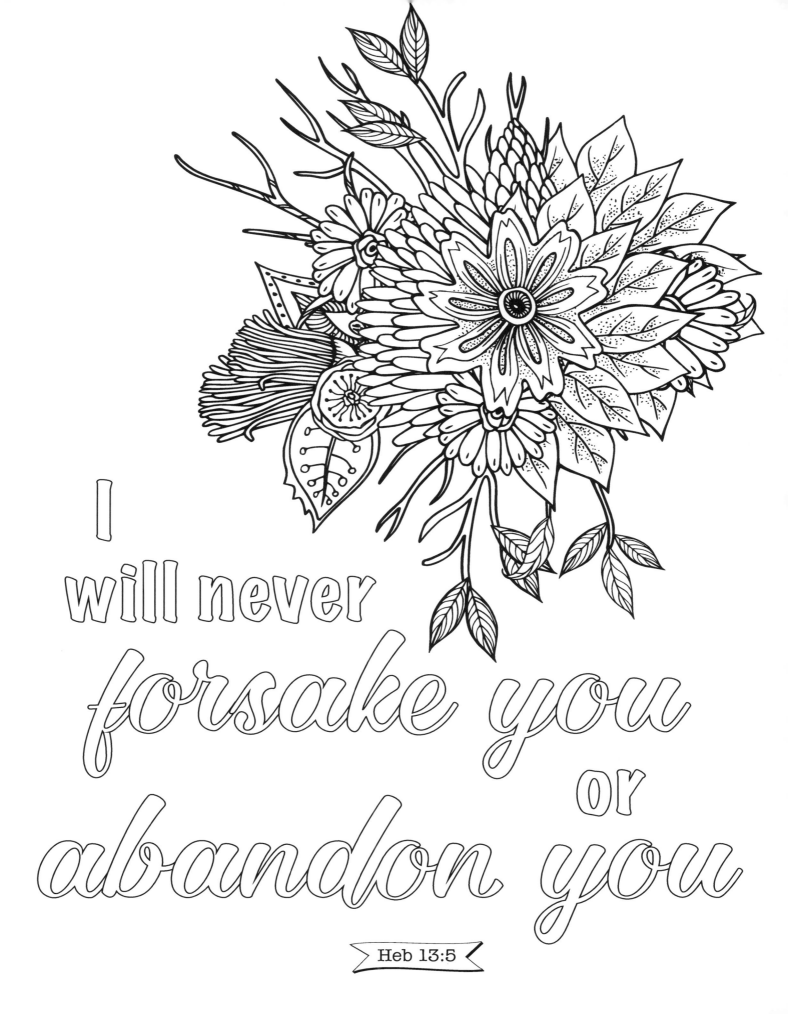

I will never forsake you or abandon you

Heb 13:5

Made in the USA
San Bernardino, CA
12 December 2016